Original title:
Wellness Habits

Copyright © 2024 Creative Arts Management OÜ
All rights reserved.

Author: Thor Castlebury
ISBN HARDBACK: 978-9916-88-302-0
ISBN PAPERBACK: 978-9916-88-303-7

Chaotic Clarity

In the storm, a whisper glows,
Through tangled thoughts, a vision grows.
Colors clash in a vibrant fight,
In chaos, we find the light.

Amidst the noise, a silence calls,
In fractured shadows, joy enthralls.
Each twist and turn a step more clear,
In chaos deep, we shed our fear.

The Invitation to Intent

Step lightly on this path of choice,
Listen close, hear your inner voice.
With every breath, the world expands,
Intent is shaped by gentle hands.

A moment's pause invites the soul,
To weave the dream, to feel the whole.
With purpose found, let spirits soar,
Embrace the now, and seek for more.

Glimmers of Groundedness

Roots dig deep in the earth below,
A quiet strength, a steady flow.
In stillness, find the sacred peace,
From chaos born, let worries cease.

The heart beats true in simple ways,
In sunlight's warmth, in twilight's gaze.
A tender touch, a knowing glance,
In groundedness, our spirits dance.

Chasing Laughter

In every moment, joy takes flight,
Chasing laughter in the night.
A silly joke, a playful tease,
In giggles shared, our minds find ease.

Through winds of whimsy, spirits rise,
In echoes bright, our hearts reprise.
With every chuckle, burdens drop,
Together, we find the laughter's stop.

Rituals of Renewal

In dawn's embrace, shadows flee,
Awakening whispers, wild and free.
Nature breathes, a gentle call,
Time to rise, and not to stall.

Stillness blooms, thoughts like trees,
Grounded roots, a mind at ease.
Moments cherished, gifts of grace,
In every breath, a sacred space.

Tides of Mindfulness

Waves of thoughts, they ebb and flow,
In each moment, calm we sow.
Breathe in deep, the world unfolds,
Feel the warmth, let comfort hold.

Quiet waters, reflecting skies,
In soft stillness, the spirit flies.
Awareness blooms, like flowers bright,
Guiding us through day and night.

A Symphony of Self-Care

Gentle notes in evening's light,
Self-love dances, pure delight.
Harmony found in simple things,
Joyfulness that kindness brings.

Melodies of rest and play,
In their rhythm, we find our way.
Serenade of heart's desire,
Fueling passions, setting fire.

Radiance in Routine

Morning rituals, sunlight gleams,
Crafting visions, chasing dreams.
Every task, a chance to find,
Beauty woven, heart aligned.

Evening calm, reflection's grace,
Each small step, a warm embrace.
In the dance of daily life,
Find the joy that cuts like knife.

Harmonies of Health

In morning light, we rise anew,
Fresh breaths of life, the dreams in view.
With gentle steps, we tread the way,
Each heartbeat sings, it's a brand new day.

Nourishing thoughts, like seeds we sow,
In gardens green, our spirits grow.
With every laugh, with every smile,
We weave our health, thread by thread, mile by mile.

Threads of Self-Care

A quiet moment, a fleeting pause,
Silencing chaos, it's what we cause.
With open hearts, we tend the soul,
We gather strength, we make it whole.

Gentle rhythms, a soothing song,
In sacred spaces, where we belong.
Each drop of love, a thread we weave,
In the fabric of life, we choose to believe.

The Symphony of Silence

In stillness deep, a whisper calls,
Echoes through the empty halls.
Where thoughts can drift like autumn leaves,
In the quiet, the heart believes.

Moments linger, wrapped in peace,
In silent songs, our worries cease.
With every breath, a solemn tune,
In the symphony, we find our boon.

Cultivating Inner Peace

In the garden of the heart, we sow,
Seeds of calm begin to grow.
With patience as our guide each day,
We find our path, we find the way.

Like waters clear, our minds can be,
Reflecting all that we can see.
With tender grace, we learn to thrive,
In the stillness, we feel alive.

Harvesting Hope

In fields of dreams, we sow today,
With seeds of thought, we pave the way.
The sun arises, bright and warm,
It nurtures strength, it shields from harm.

With every raindrop, whispers cheer,
They promise growth, they draw us near.
We gather joy, we share the light,
In unity, our hearts take flight.

A Tapestry of Themes

Threads of colors weave and sway,
Each story told, in its own way.
Patterns emerge, both bold and bright,
Reflecting truths in day and night.

With every stitch, memories blend,
From laughter's joy to sorrows penned.
Together they form a grand display,
A tapestry of life's ballet.

The Dialogues of Diligence

In silent hours, hard work speaks,
Through whispered dreams and tired cheeks.
A labor of love, a steady hand,
Each small step forms a mighty stand.

Patience blooms in the quiet hours,
Nurtured well by unseen powers.
With every struggle, barriers break,
In diligent hearts, a path we make.

Savoring Stillness

In moments hushed, the world retreats,
A gentle pause, where time completes.
The breath of nature, soft and clear,
In stillness found, we draw you near.

With open hearts, we find our space,
Embracing peace, a warm embrace.
In quietude, our souls align,
In savoring stillness, love will shine.

Refreshing the Spirit

In the morning light we rise,
With the sun, we open wide.
Nature whispers, calm and soft,
Washing worries, turning tides.

Gentle breezes dance with ease,
Carrying scents of blooming flowers.
In this moment, time will freeze,
Filling hearts with sacred powers.

Every leaf that rustles near,
Sings a song that warms the soul.
Bringing peace, dissolving fear,
In this space, we feel whole.

As we walk this path so bright,
Hand in hand, we find our way.
With the dawn, we embrace light,
In this love, forever stay.

Echoes of Joy

Laughter rings like chimes in air,
Bringing warmth to every heart.
Memories dance, a vibrant flare,
Painting life, a work of art.

In each smile, a story thrives,
Moments cherished, sweet and true.
Every glance, connection strives,
Echoes of joy in all we do.

Underneath the stars so bright,
We gather close, our spirits soar.
Sharing dreams that take to flight,
In the night, we yearn for more.

Let this melody resound,
Binding souls with golden thread.
In connection, peace is found,
As we dance where joy has led.

Crafting a Gentle Life

In the quiet of the dawn,
We weave threads of love and care.
Simple joys, like dew at dawn,
Fill our lives with hope to share.

Rays of sunlight kiss the ground,
Nature's colors softly blend.
In this peace, our hearts are found,
Crafting moments without end.

Gentle whispers guide our way,
As we gather memories sweet.
In each heartbeat, we will stay,
Creating life that feels complete.

With hands that nurture, hearts that heal,
We create a world so bright.
In each breath, our spirits feel,
Crafting dreams that take our flight.

The Bridge to Clarity

In the fog where doubts reside,
A bridge unfolds, inviting peace.
Steps of courage, hearts open wide,
Leading thoughts to sweet release.

Each stride forward, wisdom blooms,
Questions fade into the night.
Through the haze, our spirit zooms,
Guided gently to the light.

With each breath, confusion clears,
Choice and purpose weave their art.
Bridging gaps where fear appears,
Unity begins in heart.

On this path, we'll find our way,
Truth emerging from the mist.
In the dawn, we greet the day,
Clarity's embrace, a bliss.

Moments of Reflection

In silence deep, I sit and breathe,
Thoughts like whispers, softly weave.
Shadows dance in the fading light,
Finding peace in the quiet night.

Memories flutter, like fragile leaves,
Each one a story that never leaves.
Time stands still, the heart knows best,
In these moments, I find my rest.

Threads of Connection

Tangled paths that intertwine,
Hearts united, love divine.
Laughter shared, burdens eased,
In these bonds, our souls are pleased.

A gentle touch, a knowing glance,
In every moment, there's a chance.
To forge a link, to build a bridge,
In the tapestry of life, we live.

Nurtured by Nature

In the forest, whispers call,
Rustling leaves and nature's thrall.
Sunlight dapples, shadows play,
Rooted deep, I find my way.

Mountains rise, standing tall,
Rivers flow, answering the call.
In every glade, in every breeze,
Nature's touch, my heart's at ease.

Blossoms of Balance

In harmony, we find our way,
Each moment blooms, come what may.
Fragrance sweet, the earth's embrace,
In every breath, we find our place.

Winds of change, they swirl and sway,
Yet anchored roots help us stay.
With every petal, life unfolds,
In balance found, our dreams are bold.

Reflections on Rejuvenation

In the dawn's soft light, we find,
Whispers of hope, gentle and kind.
Nature unfolds, a serene grace,
Inviting us to slow our pace.

With breaths that deepen, hearts expand,
Cleansing waters kiss the land.
New beginnings in each ray,
A promise lived in bright display.

Petals bright, kissed by dew,
Echoing dreams, ever new.
In stillness, we reclaim our souls,
As nature's rhythm makes us whole.

Through every step, the journey flows,
In each embrace, the spirit grows.
Reflections gleam in quiet streams,
Awakening our brightest dreams.

The Spirit's Palette

Colors dance upon the breeze,
A vibrant splash that aims to please.
Brush strokes of life, bold and true,
In every heart, a different hue.

Each moment paints a brand-new sky,
Where laughter floats and worries fly.
From ash to gold, the shades evolve,
In the heart's canvas, we dissolve.

With every heartbeat, art unfolds,
Stories painted, yet untold.
In twilight's glow, we find our spark,
A masterpiece born from the dark.

Together we create, we share,
A mix of love that's ever rare.
In unity, our colors blend,
The spirit's palette, no end.

Patterns of Peace

In the quietude of night,
Stars weave stories, calm and bright.
Moonlight dances on the sea,
Cradling whispers of harmony.

Every breath, a gentle pause,
Nature's rhythm, without cause.
In stillness, the world aligns,
With patterns drawn by cosmic signs.

Branches sway, a soft embrace,
Guiding thoughts to sacred space.
In the tapestry of dreams,
Peaceful threads unite, it seems.

With open hearts, we carve our way,
Amongst the chaos, spirits sway.
Finding solace, hand in hand,
Patterns of peace will ever stand.

In the Embrace of Ease

In the morn, the world awakes,
With gentle winds that softly shake.
Moments linger, free of strife,
In the embrace of simple life.

Sun-kissed fields and skies so clear,
Invite the soul to draw near.
In harmony, we sway and sigh,
Underneath the endless sky.

With laughter sweet, and hearts at play,
We honor each unfolding day.
Finding joy in small delight,
Nightly stars, our guiding light.

Wrapped in ease, we dance and dream,
Life unfolds like a flowing stream.
In every heartbeat, calm is found,
In the embrace where peace abounds.

A Canvas of Choice

With colors bright and shades of grey,
Life's choices dance in light of day.
Each stroke a path, a journey made,
In every hue, adventures laid.

The brush of dreams, a gentle sway,
Guides us through the vast array.
A canvas vast, with space to roam,
Each choice, a step, a chance for home.

In shadows deep, in bright sunlight,
Our palette shifts, igniting light.
With every blend, a story spun,
A masterpiece when all is done.

So paint your dreams with vibrant care,
Each choice a chance to be laid bare.
In art of life, let spirit flow,
A canvas crafted, beauty grows.

Harvesting Happiness

Amidst the fields where sunlight glows,
We gather joy as nature grows.
With every laugh like golden grains,
Our hearts soak in the sweet refrains.

Through seasons change, we toil and play,
In simple moments, joy will stay.
We plant the seeds of laughter bright,
And watch them blossom in the light.

With hands outstretched, we reap the yield,
For happiness is a bountiful field.
In every smile and every cheer,
We harvest love, our purpose clear.

So let us dance among the rows,
And celebrate how happiness flows.
In life's embrace, we find our way,
Harvesting joy with each new day.

The Alchemy of Awareness

In quietude, the heart does peek,
Through layers deep, we learn to seek.
Awareness blooms, a golden light,
Transforming darkness into sight.

Each thought a spark, each feeling pure,
In stillness found, the soul's allure.
We blend the past with moments new,
Creating truths that feel so true.

Through mindful breath, we find our ground,
In present moments, peace is found.
With every glance, a deeper focus,
Awareness shifts, our sight uncovers.

So let us weave with gentle grace,
The alchemy of time and space.
In touch with now, we find the key,
Awareness sets our spirits free.

Serenading the Soul

In whispers soft, the nightingale,
Sings songs of love, a gentle tale.
Each note a balm for weary hearts,
In melodies, the silence parts.

The moonlight bathes the world in dreams,
As stars align in silver beams.
A serenade that knows no bounds,
In every heartbeat, beauty sounds.

With every chord, the spirit lifts,
Finding peace in nature's gifts.
In harmony, our souls entwine,
A concert rich, a love divine.

So close your eyes and take a breath,
In music's arms, we conquer death.
For in the song, we find our whole,
A serenade that stirs the soul.

The Embrace of Mindfulness

In stillness, we find peace,
The chaos starts to cease.
A gentle breath, a soft sigh,
In the moment, we learn to fly.

The world slows down, we connect,
With every thought, we reflect.
Presence wraps us like a shawl,
In silence, we hear the call.

Awareness blooms like a flower,
Growing richer by the hour.
With mindful steps, we tread light,
Illuminating the night.

Embrace the now, let go of fear,
With open hearts, we draw near.
In this dance of time and space,
We find ourselves in our place.

Moments of Melodies

In the whisper of the breeze,
A song drifts through the trees.
Notes of laughter intertwine,
Creating rhythms so divine.

Each heartbeat sings a tune,
Underneath the silver moon.
Echoes of joy, soft and sweet,
Life's melody, a vibrant beat.

Moments linger, time suspends,
Notes of love that never ends.
Harmonies shared with each gaze,
In the light, we find our blaze.

The world dances, feet take flight,
Through the day, into the night.
With every heartbeat, we express,
Life's music, our happiness.

Breathe, Believe, Become

Inhale deeply, feel the flow,
Let the waves of calmness grow.
With every breath, we find our way,
In our hearts, we choose to stay.

Belief ignites the inner flame,
A quiet whisper calls your name.
With trust, we leap into the light,
Embracing dreams that feel so right.

Become the change you wish to see,
In every thought, set your spirit free.
Transformation starts within your soul,
With every step, we become whole.

Breathe in strength, exhale doubt,
In this journey, there's no route.
Believe in love, in kindness thrive,
Become the spark, the will to strive.

Exercises in Engagement

With open eyes, we start to see,
The dance of life, in harmony.
Each smile shared, a thread of gold,
We weave connections, brave and bold.

In conversations, hearts align,
In simple acts, our souls entwine.
Listening deep, we learn to grow,
In every story, love will flow.

Embrace the moments, large and small,
Each encounter, a gift for all.
Engagement blooms in every space,
In shared experiences, we find grace.

Let's dance together, hand in hand,
Building bridges across this land.
In unity, we find our song,
In exercises, we all belong.

The Heartbeat of Harmony

In the quiet of the night, we find,
Melodies of life, intertwined.
Every whisper of the breeze,
Carries tales of ancient trees.

The stars above begin to glow,
Painting dreams in midnight's flow.
Together, hearts, we softly sing,
In the dance of joy, we take wing.

With every note, a story spun,
Unites us all, we become one.
In the rhythm, there's a grace,
Binding souls in this shared space.

Let the harmony guide our way,
Through the night, into the day.
In every heartbeat, love we trace,
Finding peace in this endless chase.

Finding Freedom in Routine

Morning light breaks through the veil,
Coffee brews, a gentle trail.
Task by task, we find our way,
Within the calm of everyday.

Routines weave a soothing thread,
Wrapping moments, gently spread.
In each chore, a chance to pause,
Find delight in simple laws.

With every step, a dance unfolds,
Within the mundane, joy beholds.
Embracing rhythms, hearts align,
In daily comforts, love we find.

Even hours may feel confined,
In the pattern, peace designed.
Freed by habits, we embrace,
The beauty found in every place.

Sunshine for the Spirit

Golden rays kiss the morning dew,
Awakening dreams in skies so blue.
Laughter dances on the breeze,
Bringing warmth to hearts at ease.

Fields of flowers start to bloom,
Painting life in vibrant plume.
Underneath the sun's embrace,
Joyful moments take their place.

Chasing shadows, letting go,
In the light, we learn to grow.
Sunshine whispers, softly ignites,
A spirit soaring to new heights.

With each beam, horizons shift,
In warmth, we find our sacred gift.
Embracing days with open heart,
In sunlight's glow, we play our part.

Anchors of Amity

In the harbor, friendship stands,
Strong as oak, with gentle hands.
Through the storms and sunny days,
We sail together, find our ways.

Trust is built on shared delights,
Through the dark and shining lights.
In laughter shared, and tears we pour,
Our bond grows deeper, evermore.

With every chapter, stories grow,
Roots entwined, we ebb and flow.
In the safe harbor, hearts reside,
With anchors firm, we turn the tide.

Together, we weather life's vast seas,
In unity, we find our ease.
Through every challenge, hand in hand,
Anchors of amity, we stand.

The Art of Stillness

In silence deep, we find our peace,
Thoughts like gentle breezes cease.
Moments stretch in quiet grace,
The world melts in this sacred space.

Breathe in calm, let worries fade,
Time slows down, a soft cascade.
Within the still, our hearts can hear,
The whispers low, so pure, sincere.

Eyes close tight, embrace the night,
Stars above, a guiding light.
In stillness, wisdom starts to flow,
A quiet heart, its truths will show.

As echoes fade, let presence stay,
In stillness, find a brighter way.
Artful moments blend and swirl,
In sacred stillness, life unfurls.

Embrace the Morning Light

Awake to dawn's warm, golden hue,
A promise bright, the day's anew.
Sunbeams dance on gentle leaves,
Nature whispers, and the heart believes.

Birds take flight, a joyful song,
In morning's arms, we all belong.
Breathe in deeply, feel the thrill,
Embrace the light, let dreams fulfill.

The world ignites with colors bold,
Fresh hopes and stories yet untold.
In morning's glow, our spirits rise,
Awash in warmth beneath the skies.

As shadows flicker, doubts will part,
In every ray, a brand new start.
Embrace the light, let shadows flee,
In every dawn, we find the key.

Mindful Steps

Each step we take, a chance to breathe,
In every moment, lessons weave.
Feet on the ground, hearts open wide,
In mindful paths, we learn to glide.

The rhythm flows, like waves on shore,
With every step, we seek for more.
Awareness blooms in what we tread,
With mindful steps, the heart is fed.

Listen close to nature's call,
As we wander, we feel it all.
Presence shines in each soft choice,
In mindful movement, hear your voice.

With every path, new sights unfold,
In simple steps, our stories told.
A journey deep within the soul,
Mindful steps make the spirit whole.

Whispers of the Heart

In twilight's glow, the heart will speak,
Soft and gentle, never weak.
Whispers dance on a silent breeze,
Carrying secrets, hopes, and pleas.

Listen close, in quiet nights,
The heart reveals its hidden lights.
In stillness, truth begins to stir,
Each whisper felt, as dreams confer.

Between the lines, our souls connect,
In every word, a sweet reflect.
Messages carried on soft sighs,
Whispers of love, beneath the skies.

So trust the whispers, let them guide,
A journey taken deep inside.
For in the heart where secrets dwell,
The whispers weave a magic spell.

Cultivating Calm

In a garden still and pure,
Where silence grows, it's sure,
With every breath, a gentle pull,
   To find a world that's full.

Nature sings a soothing song,
Where hearts can find where they belong,
With every leaf that whispers low,
   In calm, our spirits glow.

The sun dips down, the shadows play,
In twilight's glow, we find our way,
With each moment, softly held,
   In peace, our worries quelled.

Breathe in deep, let worries fade,
In this space, our fears are laid,
For in the quiet, we can see,
   That calm's the path to be free.

The Art of Mindful Moments

In morning light, a gentle pause,
We savor life, and give applause,
For tiny joys that make us whole,
In mindful living, we find our soul.

The scent of tea, the warmth it gives,
In simple acts, our spirit lives,
Each heartbeat slows, a sweet refrain,
In quiet thoughts, our peace we gain.

The world spins on, and yet we stay,
In fleeting moments, come what may,
With open hearts, we start to see,
The art of now, we must decree.

With every breath, we weave in time,
A melody, a gentle rhyme,
For life unfolds in sacred grace,
In mindful moments, we embrace.

Whispers of Harmony

In the stillness, whispers call,
Echoes of the wild's thrall,
The wind carries stories far,
Of peace, like a guiding star.

Among the trees, a softer sound,
In nature's breath, our hearts are found,
With every rustle, every sigh,
A balm for souls that long to fly.

The colors blend, the shadows dance,
In this tapestry, we find our chance,
To listen close, to understand,
The harmony in every strand.

With eyes wide open, we shall roam,
In whispers soft, we feel at home,
For in this world, where beauty lies,
In harmony, our spirit flies.

Threads of Tranquility

In quiet moments, we reside,
Where peace and stillness coincide,
With every thread, a tale is spun,
Of tranquil hearts beneath the sun.

We weave our thoughts, both soft and bright,
In gentle patterns, day and night,
For every flaw, a perfect fit,
In tranquil spaces, we won't quit.

The fabric of our dreams takes flight,
In simple joys and stars so bright,
With each connection, we create,
A world where calm and love await.

In woven threads, a story bold,
Of peace that warms, not just the cold,
For in this tapestry, we find,
Threads of tranquility entwined.

Embracing the Everyday

Morning sun on waking eyes,
Coffee brews, a sweet surprise.
Little laughs, the warmth we share,
In simple moments, love is there.

Walking paths with friends in tow,
Seasons change, yet hearts still glow.
In every task, joy we find,
Embracing days, our hearts aligned.

The Language of Light

Shadows dance, soft whispers flow,
In golden rays, stories grow.
Colors speak, the soul's delight,
A silent song, the language of light.

Reflections shimmer on the lake,
In twilight hues, the dreams we make.
Each dawn brings a brand new sight,
Echoes of hope in the morning light.

Lifting the Veil of Stress

Breathe in deep, let worries fade,
In stillness, strength is laid.
Soft embraces, a gentle touch,
Life's burdens lift, we carry less.

Nature's call, the wind's sweet song,
Reminding us where we belong.
In moments vast, our spirits mend,
Lifting the veil, finding peace within.

Reflections in Repose

Quiet nights, the moon's embrace,
Stars above weave dreams in space.
In stillness, thoughts gently flow,
Reflections dance in soft hello.

Time to ponder, drift like clouds,
In restful peace, no shouts, no crowds.
As silence cradles, worries cease,
In tranquil hearts, we find our peace.

The Essence of Elysium

In gardens where the lilies grow,
Beneath the sun's warm, golden glow.
The whispers of the softest breeze,
Awaken dreams among the trees.

A river sings its gentle tune,
Reflecting light beneath the moon.
Each petal dances, pure and bright,
In harmony with day and night.

With colors vibrant, life unfolds,
A tapestry of tales retold.
In Elysium, hearts unite,
As love ignites the world with light.

Morning Rituals

The dawn awakens, soft and pale,
A cup of warmth begins to sail.
With whispers sweet, the day unfolds,
In gentle light, the moment molds.

Birdsong flutters through the air,
A fragrant brew, without a care.
The sun peeks out, a golden sphere,
Inviting warmth, drawing us near.

With every breath, the world feels new,
A dance with time, a vibrant hue.
In sync with nature, hearts align,
As morning rituals intertwine.

Gentle Seeds of Serenity

In quiet moments, seeds are sown,
In fertile hearts, where dreams have grown.
A touch of grace, a breath of peace,
From chaos, find a sweet release.

The laughter of the brook nearby,
A lullaby beneath the sky.
With every rustle, leaves embrace,
The gentle touch of nature's grace.

In whispered sighs, the world slows down,
Where worries fade and joy is found.
In the stillness, beauty thrives,
As gentle seeds of calm arise.

The Breath of Stillness

In the heart of the silent night,
A moment grasped, tender and light.
With every pulse, the world suspends,
As time dissolves and space extends.

A fragrant hush, the air is thick,
With thoughts that pause, the clock's soft tick.
The stars above, they softly gleam,
In the vastness, we find our dream.

In stillness, wisdom starts to flow,
The breath of life, a gentle glow.
In peace, we find our sweetest song,
A quiet bond where we belong.

The Rhythm of Rediscovery

Beneath the stars, we take our stride,
In shadows deep, where dreams reside.
With every step, the past unwinds,
A melody of hope we find.

Waves of time crash on the shore,
Echoes of ages, nothing more.
Yet in the silence, hearts align,
The rhythm flows, so pure, divine.

Paths once lost now gently glow,
Mapping journeys we used to know.
Each heartbeat sings, each breath reveals,
The truth in what our spirit feels.

In whispered winds, we find our song,
A dance of souls, where we belong.
Together finding, hand in hand,
The rhythm of this promised land.

In the Focus of Fulfillment

Through the lens of morning light,
Dreams awaken, taking flight.
Every moment, crystal clear,
A canvas painted, far from fear.

With purpose strong, our hearts unite,
In every challenge, we ignite.
Together weaving tales of grace,
Unfolding paths we dare to trace.

In the stillness, visions grow,
Glimmers of what we wish to show.
With open minds and hands outstretched,
A world of wonders, deeply etched.

Fulfillment calls, a gentle breeze,
In every choice, with faith we seize.
In each heartbeat, our spirits lift,
In the focus lies our greatest gift.

Mosaic of Mindfulness

In fragments bright, our lives combine,
Colors blending, hearts align.
Moments gather, pieces fit,
A tapestry of life, well-lit.

With mindful breaths, we pause to see,
The beauty in simplicity.
Each thought a brushstroke, light and free,
Creating art in harmony.

In laughter shared and sorrows borne,
In every bite of bread, each thorn.
A mosaic built through love and care,
In every glance, a story's flare.

Together stitching, day by day,
A vibrant quilt that will not fray.
In stillness find the joy we've made,
A mindful life, in colors displayed.

A Symphony of Simplicity

In gentle notes, the quiet hum,
A melody that beckons, come.
With softest whispers, life presents,
A symphony of purest scents.

Each breath a chord, familiar tune,
In nature's lap, beneath the moon.
With measured steps, we walk in grace,
Finding peace in every space.

Embrace the stillness, let it flow,
Release the weight that burdens so.
The sound of laughter, birds in flight,
In simplicity, we find our light.

In quiet moments, wisdom grows,
In every heart, a rhythm flows.
A symphony, sweet and sublime,
Unraveling the threads of time.

Threads of Resilience

In shadows deep, we find our way,
With threads of hope that gently sway.
Each stitch a story, strong and true,
Holding us close, pulling us through.

When storms arise, we stand as one,
Our hearts united, battles won.
Through trials faced, we rise and shine,
With courage woven, hearts entwined.

In every tear, a lesson learned,
With every fear, a fire burned.
The fabric's strength, in love is sewn,
A tapestry of strength that we've grown.

Together we weave, with hands held tight,
In the darkest hours, we find our light.
Resilience blooms, in silence found,
A symphony of hope, forever sound.

The Dawn of Dedication

As night gives way to morning's glow,
The path ahead begins to show.
With every step, a promise made,
In dedication, fears will fade.

The sun ascends with golden rays,
Illuminating heartfelt ways.
With passion's fire, dreams ignite,
In every challenge, we find our might.

Through trials faced and hurdles crossed,
We'll find the gains when we perceive the cost.
With steadfast hearts, our spirits soar,
In dedication, we'll seek for more.

Together we strive, in unity bright,
Guided by the stars, we chase the light.
In every moment, our hearts aligned,
The dawn of dedication we will find.

Embracing the Now

In the whisper of the breeze, we feel,
Moments fleeting, yet truly real.
With open hearts, we take it in,
Embracing life where love begins.

The ticking clock, a gentle muse,
In every heartbeat, we choose to lose.
To past regrets and future fears,
In this present, joy appears.

Through laughter shared and tears we cry,
In simple moments, we learn to fly.
With each breath taken, we rise anew,
Embracing the now, just me and you.

In stillness found, we ground our souls,
Together complete, we find our roles.
With open arms, let life unfold,
In embracing now, our hearts are bold.

Celebrating Simplicities

In every sunrise, a promise pure,
In simple joys, our hearts allure.
A cup of tea, a gentle smile,
In these moments, life's worth the while.

A child's laughter, a bird in flight,
The quiet stillness of the night.
With every breath, we take it in,
Celebrating life, where dreams begin.

With nature's grace, the world we know,
In simple pleasures, our spirits grow.
A friend's embrace, a story shared,
In these small things, we feel prepared.

Let's hold these moments, let them stay,
In life's simplicity, we find our way.
With open hearts and eyes so bright,
We celebrate simplicity, our guiding light.

Echoes of Balance

In the hush of twilight's glow,
Whispers dance, both high and low.
Nature's song, a gentle call,
Harmony reigns, embracing all.

Waves of silence blend and sway,
Life's cadence finds its way.
Silent moments, soft and sweet,
Balance flows in heart's heartbeat.

Stars align in cosmic streams,
Living bright within our dreams.
Echoes of a world so wide,
In stillness, we learn to guide.

Together we seek, never part,
Finding peace within the heart.
In each breath, the world we trace,
Echoes whisper, a sacred space.

Dancing with Delight

Beneath the sun, the flowers sway,
A joyful tune, the heart's ballet.
Colors blend in vibrant flight,
Life awakens, pure delight.

Laughter sparkles in the air,
Wings of hope, a light to share.
Every step, a rhythmic beat,
In this dance, we find our feet.

Gentle breezes lift our souls,
Spinning dreams, we lose control.
With each turn, our spirits rise,
In this moment, joy defies.

Hands reach out, together we twine,
In the dance, our hearts align.
With wonder, we boldly ignite,
The world spins, in pure delight.

The Garden of Grace

Where blossoms open, softly wide,
In fragrant air, our dreams reside.
Gentle waves of warmth and light,
In this garden, all feels right.

Paths of color, rich and deep,
Nature's promise, ours to keep.
Every petal, soft embrace,
In this haven, we find grace.

Morning dew, like diamonds shine,
Whispers of the divine.
Moments cherished, tender space,
In the stillness, find our place.

Together here, we bloom and grow,
In the love that we both know.
The garden thrives, a sacred space,
Within, we find our endless grace.

Paths to Inner Peace

Whispers call along the way,
Inviting hearts to pause and stay.
Gentle trails, both calm and clear,
In this journey, we draw near.

Mountains high and valleys low,
Nature's breath, a soothing flow.
In the stillness, minds release,
Finding strength in inner peace.

Through the forest, shadows play,
Guiding us to light of day.
Every step, a chance to find,
Harmony within the mind.

In the quiet, wisdom grows,
Like a river, life bestows.
Together on these paths we tread,
Toward the light where hope is fed.

Savoring Each Breath

Inhale the whispers of the dawn,
A moment holds the world at bay.
Exhale the worries we have drawn,
In this stillness, find your way.

Beneath the sky so vast and blue,
Each breath a gift, a chance to feel.
A dance with time, both old and new,
Embrace the now; let it reveal.

The pulse of life in every part,
In silence, hear the softest sound.
A symphony begins to start,
As heart and breath together bound.

In every sigh, a story lives,
A rhythm known, yet never chained.
To breathe is all that nature gives,
In each exhale, joy is gained.

Finding Joy in Ordinary

Morning light spills on the floor,
A simple cup of tea in hand.
The world awakens, who could ask for more?
In the quiet, life is grand.

A stroll through streets, a smile shared,
The laughing child in bright sunlight.
These fleeting moments, unprepared,
They weave our hearts in sheer delight.

The rustle of leaves in the breeze,
The warmth of laughter all around.
A heart that dances, free to seize
The joy that's buried, yet profound.

In every corner, light will show,
The beauty in the day-to-day.
Finding joy where love can grow,
In mundane hours, we find our way.

Colors of the Mind

A whispering palette on my canvas bright,
Each stroke a memory, vivid and pure.
Dreams unravel under the soft moonlight,
A tapestry of thoughts that endure.

Hues of laughter mix with the gray,
The vivid reds of passion and strife.
Blues of calm in a world that sways,
Colors blend in the art of life.

Shadows linger where fears reside,
Yet, golden beams pierce the night's deep shroud.
In the spectrum, pain and joy collide,
Creating beauty, fierce and loud.

Brush in hand, I capture the scene,
A kaleidoscope of dreams untold.
In the frenzy, I find serene,
The colors of the heart unfold.

The Heart's Sanctuary

In the depths of silent night,
Whispers linger, soft and low.
A place where dreams take gentle flight,
The heart's own haven, there we go.

Wrapped in warmth, where shadows play,
A refuge from the clamor loud.
In stillness, life finds its own way,
A sacred space beneath the cloud.

Each secret hope, a tender thread,
Woven tightly in love's embrace.
In this sanctuary, we are led,
To face the world with quiet grace.

Here, sorrows melt like morning dew,
The pulse of peace within us flows.
In the heart's sanctuary, we renew,
A beacon that forever glows.

Dawn's Gentle Whispers

In twilight's arms, the stars disappear,
Soft hues emerge, the sky draws near.
Bird songs blend with the hush of night,
Dawn breaks gently, painting in light.

Clouds dance softly, in shades of pink,
The world awakens, begins to think.
Whispers of warmth in the morning air,
Hope ignites as dreams take care.

Golden rays kiss the earth awake,
Each moment precious, memories we make.
Nature beckons with a tender sigh,
Dawn's embrace, the heart's reply.

With every day, a chance once more,
To spread our wings and to explore.
In this soft glow, life resumes its song,
In dawn's gentle whispers, we all belong.

The Sweetness of Slowness

In moments cherished, time stands still,
Savoring life's taste, a gentle thrill.
With every breath, the heart aligns,
In the sweetness of slowness, the spirit shines.

Each petal unfolds, kissed by the dew,
Nature's ballet, a tranquil view.
The world rushes past, but we remain,
Finding joy in the simplest refrain.

Let the clock tick slowly, let shadows play,
In quiet corners, we find our way.
A cup of tea, the sun's soft beam,
In the sweetness of slowness, we dream.

Life's fleeting dance, a gentle grace,
In every heartbeat, we find our place.
With open hearts, let stillness dwell,
In the sweetness of slowness, all is well.

Declarations of Determination

Voices rise with unwavering might,
Chasing visions, igniting the night.
With every challenge, we stand tall,
Declarations echo, we won't fall.

In the face of doubt, we find our way,
A fire within, guiding each day.
Through storms and shadows, we will strive,
In declarations, our dreams revive.

Together united, hand in hand,
We'll carve our path, take a stand.
With grit and grace, we'll face the fight,
Declarations of hope, our shining light.

Through the battles, we boldly tread,
Determined hearts, our fears shed.
With strength like rivers, we will flow,
Declarations of determination, let us grow.

Balancing Acts

In life's great circus, we walk the line,
Juggling dreams, all sacred and fine.
Each breath a pause, a chance to see,
The delicate art of harmony.

Twirling hopes and fears like a dance,
In every step, we take our chance.
Holding tight to what we love,
Balancing acts, like stars above.

In fleeting moments, joy and pain,
We find our strength through life's refrain.
Ebb and flow, like waves at sea,
In balancing acts, we find melody.

Through ups and downs, we'll stand our ground,
In the heart of chaos, peace is found.
With every challenge, we'll react,
In this grand life, we learn to act.

Grounded in Gratitude

In morning light, I wake and breathe,
Thankful for the day ahead,
For every moment I can seize,
And every word that's softly said.

The laughter shared, the hands that hold,
The stories stitched with threads of care,
In simple joys, my heart unfolds,
In gratitude, I'm rich and rare.

With each sunset, I find my peace,
Reflecting on the love I've known,
In gratitude, my soul's release,
A bond through which I've always grown.

In every step, I find my way,
With grateful heart, I navigate,
Embracing life, come what may,
In gratitude, I celebrate.

Flowing Through Nature

Whispers of wind through emerald leaves,
Nature's voice, a gentle song,
In every path that nature weaves,
I feel my spirit grow more strong.

Mountains rise, their peaks so high,
Rivers dance, they twist and twine,
Clouds drift softly in the sky,
In this magic, I align.

From forests deep to oceans wide,
Each step a blessing, rich and pure,
In nature's arms, I find my guide,
A flowing peace, a heart secure.

The sun will set, the stars will gleam,
In every shadow, light will show,
Through nature's realm, I chase my dream,
For in this flow, my essence grows.

The Dance of Balance

In every step, I find the grace,
A dance between the dark and light,
With gentle rhythm, I embrace,
The harmony that feels just right.

The pull of work, the need for rest,
In subtle swings, I find my way,
With every choice, I feel the best,
As life unfolds, come what may.

The joy of laughter, moments still,
In every heartbeat, balance sways,
With open heart, I find the thrill,
In the dance of life's many ways.

As moonlight meets the morning sun,
In ebb and flow, my spirit soars,
In balance found, I've just begun,
To dance with life, to seek and explore.

Radiate Positivity

With every dawn, I choose to shine,
A light within, a spark so bright,
In thoughts and words, I intertwine,
The power of uplifting light.

Each kindness shared, a seed I sow,
In hearts around, it blooms and grows,
With every smile, I let it flow,
The warmth of love that overflows.

Through trials faced, I lift my gaze,
Embracing hope, I rise anew,
In vibrant hues, I find my ways,
To radiate the bright and true.

In every moment, I will find,
The beauty in both near and far,
To shine my light, and be so kind,
Radiating joy, my guiding star.

Awaken the Senses

In the morning light, the birds sing,
Soft whispers of the wind take wing.
Bright blooms open with the sun's touch,
Nature's call awakens us so much.

The scent of dew on fresh green grass,
A gentle breeze, as moments pass.
Colors dance in a painter's dream,
Every detail speaks, or so it seems.

Taste of ripe fruit, sweet and bright,
A world of flavors, pure delight.
An earthy richness in each bite,
Waking senses, sparking light.

Touch the petals, feel the earth,
Every texture, a moment's worth.
In this embrace, the heart finds home,
Awakened senses, free to roam.

Resilience in Routine

In the rhythm of dawn, we rise anew,
Stepping forward with a steadfast view.
Footprints mark the path we tread,
In familiar places, courage is bred.

The coffee brews, a comforting sound,
In the mundane, strength is found.
Simple tasks, each one a stone,
Building bridges, we stand alone.

Through the cycles of day and night,
Routine wraps us in soft light.
In predictable paths, we flourish,
Resilience blooms, our spirits nourish.

With every step, we learn to trust,
In habits formed, we find what's just.
In the weave of life, strength is sewn,
Resilience born from seeds we've grown.

Seeds of Calm

In quiet moments, stillness grows,
A gentle whisper, soft as snow.
Plant seeds of calm in troubled ground,
In the heart's garden, peace is found.

Breathe in deep, let worries fade,
In tranquil waters, shade is laid.
Each breath a chance to start anew,
Nurturing the soul, fresh as dew.

With each sunset, let go the day,
Stars will light a softer way.
The quiet night wraps dreams in grace,
Seeds of calm in night's embrace.

In harmony, our minds can rest,
In pause, we find our very best.
With patience, love will gently bloom,
In the silence, we find room.

The Path to Wholeness

Along the path where shadows play,
We find our truth, day by day.
Footsteps echo in silent grace,
Embracing all, we find our place.

Each twist and turn, a lesson learned,
Through valleys low and hills we've turned.
In the journey, pieces unite,
A tapestry woven, vibrant and bright.

Emotions rise like the morning tide,
In each heartbeat, we love and guide.
With open hearts, we heal the soul,
In this journey, we become whole.

Through every struggle, we arise,
In the dance of life, we realize.
The path unfolds with every step,
Wholeness found in love's adept.

The Compass of Contentment

In the quiet heart of night,
Dreams take flight, gentle and bright.
Stars whisper secrets, soft and clear,
Guiding souls to what they hold dear.

With every breath, a moment's grace,
Finding joy in a simple space.
The world slows down, worries relent,
Peace resides where hearts are content.

In laughter shared and love's embrace,
Life unfurls at its own pace.
The compass spins, but always stays,
Pointing to home in many ways.

Through storms that come and shadows cast,
Hold onto light, let darkness pass.
The journey flows, a sacred quest,
Within our hearts, we find our rest.

Whirling Wisdom

On the dance floor of the mind,
Ideas swirl, vast and unconfined.
Wisdom whispers, soft yet loud,
In the chaos, brightly proud.

Lessons learned from pain and cheer,
Each twirl reveals what's held dear.
Like leaves that drift in autumn air,
Thoughts take flight, unbound, aware.

In the silence, wisdom grows,
Through the clutter, clarity flows.
Embrace the dance, lose the fear,
Life's grand tapestry draws near.

With every spin, a truth unfolds,
In the heart, a story told.
So whirling minds forever seek,
In the rhythm, we find our speak.

Aroma of Affection

In the garden where memories bloom,
Sweet scents linger, dispelling gloom.
Each hug, a petal, soft and pure,
Binding hearts with love's allure.

Like morning coffee, warm and bold,
Aroma of affection, pure gold.
Through seasons change, a fragrant trace,
Of moments shared, in love's embrace.

In laughter's echo, whispers sweet,
A symphony of hearts, a rhythmic beat.
With every breath, we grow and weave,
The scent of love, we won't deceive.

So let us cherish each tender hour,
And let love blossom, a radiant flower.
In the air, let kindness spread,
In the aroma of words unsaid.

Alight with Awareness

In the dawn's gentle light, we rise,
Eyes wide open to the skies.
Each moment pulses, alive and bright,
Awareness beckons, a guiding light.

Through whispers of the morning breeze,
Nature sings, inviting ease.
Each breath a gift, so pure, so true,
Alight with awareness, we start anew.

As shadows dance and daylight grows,
Feel the rhythm, where wisdom flows.
The world around us starts to sway,
In the light of now, we find our way.

So pause a while, let the stillness in,
Breathe deeply, let the magic begin.
For in each heartbeat, life's essence stands,
Alight with awareness, in open hands.

The Dance of Daily Joy

In morning light, we rise and shine,
With laughter sweet, and hearts entwined.
Each simple task, a chance to play,
In sunny skies, we greet the day.

With every breath, a spark ignites,
In moments shared, our spirit flights.
Together we sway, in life's ballet,
Embracing joy, come what may.

As twilight falls, the colors blend,
In whispers soft, our hearts descend.
In quietude, we find our song,
In daily joy, where we belong.

So let us move, in rhythm true,
With every step, our hearts renew.
In dance we find, a love so clear,
In daily joy, we hold it dear.

Pillars of Vitality

Roots run deep, in soil rich,
Through storms and sun, we find the stitch.
With every breath, a pulse we feel,
In life's embrace, we learn to heal.

Branches stretch, to kiss the sky,
In vibrant hues, the spirits fly.
Each leaf a dream, a hope, a chance,
In nature's rhythm, we find our dance.

Together stand, our hearts aligned,
In strength we grow, with love designed.
Through trials faced, we rise anew,
In pillars strong, we find our view.

So cherish roots, and reach for light,
With every dawn, embrace the fight.
In vibrant life, we plant our seed,
In pillars bold, we fulfill our need.

The Journey to Joyfulness

Step by step, we share the way,
In laughter's echo, we find our play.
With open hearts, we chase the dream,
In every moment, we find the gleam.

Through valleys low, and mountains high,
In every tear, a chance to fly.
With every smile, we light the path,
In joyfulness, we find the math.

As shadows fade, the sun will rise,
With grateful hearts, we claim the prize.
In friendship's bond, we rise and soar,
In journey shared, we crave for more.

So hold my hand, let's dance along,
In joyful steps, we'll sing our song.
With every turn, a tale to weave,
In joyfulness, we learn to believe.

Tuning into Tranquility

In silent woods, where whispers greet,
The heart finds peace, and stillness sweet.
With every breath, we slow the race,
In tranquil moments, we find our place.

Soft breezes sigh, through ancient trees,
In nature's hold, we find our ease.
Every leaf, a gentle sigh,
In calm's embrace, our spirits fly.

The stars above, a guide so bright,
In quietness, they paint the night.
With open eyes, we see the glow,
In tranquil thoughts, our minds will flow.

So take a breath, and feel the still,
In gentle waves, let worries chill.
With every moment, peace will grow,
In tuning in, we learn to know.

Nourish the Soul

In quiet corners, wisdom waits,
To plant the seeds of gentle fate.
With every breath, a bond we weave,
In silence, we learn to believe.

Nature whispers, soft and clear,
It teaches us to hold what's dear.
With every touch of sun and rain,
Our hearts expand, we rise again.

In moments shared, our spirits bloom,
A dance of joy, dispelling gloom.
Together, we embrace the whole,
In every heartbeat, nourish soul.

With laughter bright, and love's embrace,
We find our peace, our sacred space.
Through storms and trials, we shall stroll,
Forever seeking to nourish soul.

Breathe Deep

Inhale the calm, exhale the strife,
A gentle rhythm, the pulse of life.
Each breath a gift, a chance to start,
Awakened senses, open heart.

The world outside may roar and rush,
But here, we find our sacred hush.
With every moment, cherish grace,
In quietude, we find our place.

Breathe deep the essence of the now,
Let go of burdens, take a vow.
To cherish time, the fleeting days,
In every breath, the spirit sways.

So pause and feel the life within,
In stillness, let the journey begin.
With every inhale, let worries flee,
In the heart's calm, simply breathe deep.

Live Free

In the wild, where dreams take flight,
We dance beneath the stars at night.
No chains to bind, no fears to hold,
In laughter's warmth, the heart turns bold.

Each sunrise brings a chance anew,
To break the mold, to push on through.
With open arms, we greet the day,
As nature whispers, "Come, let's play."

The roads may twist, the paths may bend,
But through adventure, spirits mend.
With courage rising, we explore,
In every heartbeat, we find more.

So let us roam, both brave and free,
In every moment, just let it be.
For life's a song, a joyous spree,
With open hearts, we choose to live free.

Serenity in Motion

The world spins fast, yet here we glide,
In harmony where peace resides.
With every step, we flow and sway,
In rhythms soft, we find our way.

The gentle breeze, a guiding hand,
It lifts us up, helps us to stand.
With mindful grace, we touch the ground,
In silence sweet, our hearts resound.

Time slows down, the chaos fades,
In tranquil moments, love cascades.
Each motion felt, each sigh released,
We dance together, joy increased.

So let us move, a steady beat,
In every pulse, find solace sweet.
With open hearts, let feelings flow,
In serenity, our spirits glow.

Rituals of Renewal

In morning's light, we greet our day,
With gratitude, we find our way.
A cup of warmth, a moment still,
In simple joys, the heart can fill.

With every season, change unfolds,
In nature's dance, the story told.
A walk in woods, beneath the trees,
In every shadow, find the breeze.

We gather strength from what we know,
In rituals, let the spirit grow.
Light a candle, whisper a prayer,
In sacred spaces, love is there.

So pause, reflect, renew your soul,
Embrace the warmth, let laughter roll.
Through life's embrace and its sweet call,
In rituals deep, we find our all.

Milton Keynes UK
Ingram Content Group UK Ltd.
UKHW051811101024
449294UK00007BA/63